Enigmas
Celtic

Cunning reader, can you solve these games and enigmas designed to put your mental acuity to the test?

Contents

It all adds up

Help Goulven score 50 points exactly with only 3 throws at these targets.

Solution p. 149.

Only blue

— Listen very closely, apprentice druid, and get ready to stir up your grey matter.

You see before you the Cromlech of Pou-Niairisson, the deep heart of Celtic culture. Sixty blue stones arranged in a huge circle. But these blue stones that appear to be all the same from far away may reveal certain differences up close.

The problem, my young friend, is that you mustn't confuse dolerite, a magma-based rock, and rhyolite, a lava-based rock. If they were right under your nose, you would see that the dolerite is flecked with little spots of very pale pink.

But they aren't right under your nose, and all you see is blue ... So let's use a little logic. At least one of these blue stones is dolerite. On the other hand, if you were to choose two blue stones at random from among these megaliths, I can guarantee you that one of them is rhyolite.

So tell me, apprentice druid, how many dolerites are there in the Cromlech, and how many rhyolites?

Solution p. 152.

Celtic cross

Put the five missing pearls on this Celtic cross back in their place, on the understanding that a circle, vertical or horizontal never contains two pearls of the same shape.

Three of the pearls have already been placed.

Solution p. 147.

Debris

Eight pieces from some drawings of Celtic crosses have been found.
One complete cross can be reconstructed using five of the pieces.

Which pieces are left over?

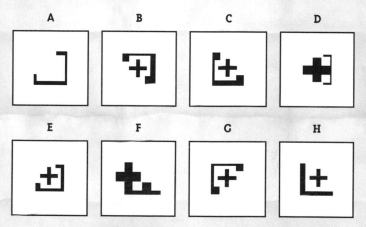

Solution p. 132.

7

The influence of oral hygiene on cutting menhirs

These five propositions are true:

1. No druid without a sagum drinks fermented barley.
2. No druid without a beard cuts menhirs.
3. Druids with moustaches drink fermented barley.
4. No sagum-wearing druid has bad breath.
5. Bearded druids have moustaches.

Do druids with bad breath cut menhirs?

Solution p. 152.

Change

A short lesson from the great druid Cathbad:

'I have two coins in my purse. If I triple the value of my first coin, I have the total value of the coins in my purse. And twice the total value of the coins in my purse is 12.'

How much do the coins in his purse add up to?

First coin  =?

Second coin =?

Solution p. 139.

The four daughters of druid O'March

Druid O'March's four daughters were all born on 28 February — it's more convenient for celebrating birthdays, after all. Marmee O'March, whose sense of practicality needs no proof, makes an enormous grain cake for the occasion, and it's done with until the next year.

On 28 February of this particular year, the youngest daughter, Amy, the one who sleeps with a menhir on her nose to make it straighter, makes this very wise remark: 'Four years ago, there were three times fewer candles than today'.

How old are the sisters today?

Solution p. 154.

Amicable divorce

— This is a riddle for a beginner, O'Gorilh my friend, and I have no doubt that you are ready to shoot back your answer … otherwise, I'm not sure we will be able to go on much further together:

> *Believe us or not*
> *We can live together*
> *For a whole lifetime*
> *And yet separate*
> *(Without getting upset)*
> *For a yes or a no*

What on earth could it be?
Solution p. 156.

The forged sickle

A druid from the Bellovaci tribe owns a small collection of nine golden sickles, which have been made throughout his life by the same craftsman, all poured into the same mould, exactly the same size, exactly the same weight … in principle!

Because on this particular occasion, having recited his incantations over the sacred mistletoe, instead of rain, hail has come crashing down on the fields of barley. The druid is convinced: the sickle he chose at random from his collection and used to cut the sacred mistletoe is defective, and his craftsman supplier or one of his employees has, at some point or other, been dishonest with him.

But which sickle? After taking one at random — as he always does — and used it, our druid has put the sickle back into his sickle bag in no particular order. As much as he takes out each sickle and weighs it in his hands, one after the other, he isn't able to identify which one contains less gold: as objects they are too awkwardly balanced and any difference in weight is too small.

Fortunately, the Bellovaci tribe has passed down, from generation to generation, an ingenious object made up of two trays and a beam that allows weights to be compared: they call it 'a set of scales'. Tradition relates that the scales' ingenious inventor was a cyclops, a monstrous being who lived back in the mists of time in a local cave in the area, the Roberval cave. He was called Nobody, like all cyclops, so the invention is called the Scales of Nobody.

This venerable object is only brought out on exceptional occasions and, so that it isn't worn out, it is only allowed to be used for two weighings at a time.

How can our druid go about eliminating the bad sickle, using the Scales of Nobody (of Roberval)?

Solution p. 155.

Caesar sabotaged

A Celtic patriot has stumbled by chance on a copy of the texts that Caesar dedicates to his ancestors in *Commentaries on the Gallic War*. Vexed, he scrambles up the letters of certain words to prevent the text from being easily understood.

Can you decipher the anagrams to restore the meaning of the text?

Caesar had every reason to suppose that Gaul was FDIAPCEI. But when RSCSSUA, needing grain to DVEROIP for his troops, sent out EESSMSIIAR amongst the neighbouring Celtic states to demand a UNINOTIOCTRB, the EETVIN revolted. They imprisoned the Roman envoys. It has to be said that this TATES was by far the most WELFROPU on the whole sea ASCTO. They had a very great number of ISHPS, which they used for sailing to NABRTII; they surpassed other OSEEPLP in their knowledge and experience of VIOAGAITNN; and as ERORNSTCLOL of the few PRTOS scattered along that stormy and open sea, they extracted SUTIRTEB from all who sailed in that OIEGNR. They thus gave their neighbours the signal to TROVLE. They agreed to SDANT up to the Romans and act THRGTEOE. A very proud people, they chose to continue in that TRYELIB which they had received from their ETCSSARON rather than endure the yoke of LYSREVA under the SEVIDNRA. But CRASAE could not accept this and prepared to wage war.

Solution p. 131.

14

Caesar had every reason to suppose that Gaul was _ _ _ _ _ _ _ _.
But when _ _ _ _ _ _ _, needing grain to _ _ _ _ _ _ _ for his
troops, sent out _ _ _ _ _ _ _ _ _ _ amongst the neighbouring
Celtic states to demand a _ _ _ _ _ _ _ _ _ _ _ _ _, the _ _ _ _ _ _ _
revolted. They imprisoned the Roman envoys. It has to be said that
this _ _ _ _ _ was by far the most _ _ _ _ _ _ _ _ on the whole sea
_ _ _ _ _. They had a very great number of _ _ _ _ _, which they
used for sailing to _ _ _ _ _ _ _; they surpassed other _ _ _ _ _ _ _
in their knowledge and experience of _ _ _ _ _ _ _ _ _ _, and, as
_ _ _ _ _ _ _ _ _ _ _ of the few _ _ _ _ _ scattered along that
stormy and open sea, they extracted _ _ _ _ _ _ _ _ from all who
sailed in that _ _ _ _ _ _. They thus gave their neighbours the
signal to _ _ _ _ _ _ _. They agreed to _ _ _ _ _ up to the Romans
and act _ _ _ _ _ _ _ _ _. A very proud people, they chose to
continue in that _ _ _ _ _ _ _ which they had received from their
_ _ _ _ _ _ _ _ _, rather than endure the yoke of _ _ _ _ _ _ _
under the _ _ _ _ _ _ _ _.
But _ _ _ _ _ _ could not accept this and prepared to wage war.

Dice game

Laorans and Paskal are playing with dice. Laorans has thrown his two dice but doesn't show them. He announces:
'The value of my second die is equal to twice the value of my first die.'

Paskal has thrown his first die but doesn't show it and says:
'If I throw my second die and get a 6, I am sure to at least equal your score.'

How can he say this with such certainty?

Solution p. 135.

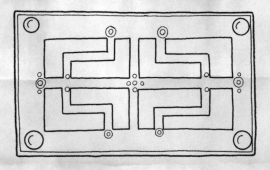

Cairn

A burial chamber has been covered with stones, forming a cairn. Archaeologists are excavating the site, but don't want to destroy the inner walls of the chamber. They have discovered a sort of site plan, but it is in code. You have to help them work out the layout.

Colour in the walls of the grid, on the principle that the number in each square indicates how many sides of the square it is in are filled in. The wall plan will thus appear.

Solution p. 126.

0	0	2	1	2	1
2	2	2	1	2	1
1	1	1	2	1	1
2	2	1	2	1	1
1	2	2	0	2	2
0	1	1	0	1	0

Show me the money

A Biturige coining workshop employs 40 enamellers, who strike bronze coins and decorate them with red enamel.
These 40 enamellers produce 400 coins in 4 days.

But a nasty illness — the result, it is sometimes claimed, of Armorican permissiveness — hits the whole Celtic world, affecting the financial sector in particular, leading to sudden and unruly fluctuations, to the point where the manager of the workshop is thinking of sending half of his employees packing.

Without speeding up the work rate, how many coins can 20 enamellers produce in 2 days?

Solution p. 157.

The home of the true

Heed me well, druid apprentice, and think on the question posed to you by a druid of a respectable age who seeks to transmit his ancient and venerable wisdom to you — not a given, apparently …

This is my riddle:

In order to be respected
I must first be given
But who gives me more than once
can never be a gentleman.

What on earth could it be?

Solution p. 157.

19

Embroidery

Work out what pattern Viviane is embroidering on her tunic.
We have given you the sequence of points to fill in (starting from the left of each row and the top of each column): for example, 3 1 in a row means that, starting from the left of the row, there will be 3 filled-in points in a row, then 1 filled-in point by itself. It's up to you to work out, by cross-checking the rows and columns, where they are …   *Solution p. 120.*
Example:

3   1

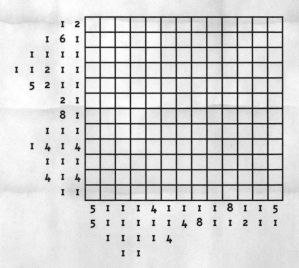

The captain's age

The druid Mac Rhoss Efal, a Caledonian from the Damnonii tribe, had to cross the Clyde to attend a sacred ceremony on the other side of the river, 20 leagues downstream. Forty others were crowded on the riverbank and the bargeman on his boat warned them that he could only take 30: the others would have to wait until the shuttle returned and so would be crossing later.

'I am the druid Mac Rhoss Efal, and I am expected at a sacred ceremony, you have to give me priority to get on the boat.'
'Now now, no use getting high and mighty, you can queue up like everyone else!' retorted the captain of the boat.
'You may have no respect for the religion of your forefathers', replied the druid, exasperated, 'but at least have a little consideration for your elders! Do you realise, young whippersnapper, that given my current age of 60, I am five times the age you were when I was the age you are now!'

How old is the captain?

Solution p. 157.

Family numbers

The Mac Roch'Twahopinsojenlaivlechel family has as many daughters as the seven dwarves and each of these daughters (who are as numerous as the seven dwarves) has a brother. Including the mother, whose name is not Snow White, plus the father — about whom all we know is that he inherited from his own father the proud name of Mac Roch'Twahopinsojenlaivlechel, a little long, but not so bad in those faraway times when there were no social security forms to fill out — how many members does this family have?

Solution p. 158.

Necklaces

Work out how much each of these kinds of precious stone is worth,
if each necklace is worth 200 sestertii. *Solution p. 150.*

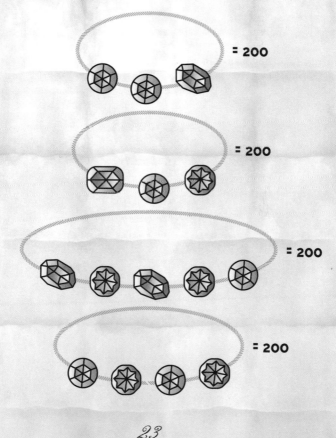

= 200

= 200

= 200

= 200

23

TREASURE

Six Celtic coins are hidden in this meadow, marked out in a grid, for which we have given you the plan and the following clues:

• There are no coins in the squares with numbers in them.
• The numbers in the squares indicate the number of adjacent squares containing a coin.
• There is only one coin per square.

Examples:

Solution p. 179.

for the table below, the possible solutions are:

Complete the grid

				I
I		I		
		2		3
	I			3
I	I		2	

Giant!

'It weighs more than thirty of those horrible war monsters that a distant ancestor of mine, a great traveller, saw in action when Alexander's horsemen fought King Porus's mahouts, called *elephants*', declared the old druid, bowing down before the Kerloas Menhir.

And he continued as follows:

'Don't go thinking that it was men like yourself who were able to transport these huge stones, even less lift them, and you'll have a hard time finding any trace of a path around here! It was Gargan the giant who put it here, with the same ease as he scattered all the blocks of granite around in the fields of Plouarzel. It was his way of thanking the local people for serving him, to honour him and to assuage his hunger, a foul porridge …'

'Yes, Mr Sceptic, it was no more difficult for him than … than … I know, than tracing a circle on this piece of leather, representing a menhir and then, without the pencil leaving the surface, without once lifting my nib, drawing another circle that's quite separate from the first one! You'll find no path here either!'

How can the druid go about doing this?

Solution p. 158.

Half True

— There is, apprentice druid, a faraway land, further away than the Highlands, further than Hibernia, a strange and fantastical land where half of 9 equals 4.

How could such a thing be possible?

Solution p. 159.

You can't count on the wind

— Stop right there, you miserable wretch, don't move a muscle! You almost stepped on the twigs the crow has dropped at the foot of the sacred willow tree. Pause for a moment and consider the message of truth it sends us:

$$\textbf{XIII} - \textbf{VIII} = \textbf{II} \times \textbf{I}$$

Hm! I agree, the mathematics is dubious ... no doubt the wind has moved one of the twigs!

Can you put it back in the right place, so the formula is correct again?

Solution p. 153.

Training

Five young Celtic warriors are practising their handling of various weapons.

For each warrior, you need to work out his weapon, age, and how long he trains for each week.

	Bow	Sword	Axe	Lance	Club	16hrs/week	18hrs/week	20hrs/week	22hrs/week	24hrs/week	17 years	18 years	19 years	20 years	21 years
Alarig															
Beltram															
Gwennole															
Malo															
Winog															
17 years															
18 years															
19 years															
20 years															
21 years															
16hrs/week															
18hrs/week															
20hrs/week															
22hrs/week															
24hrs/week															

Solution p. 148.

Clues:

Malo is 1 year older than the warrior practising archery, but 1 year younger than the one training 22 hours per week.

The axe specialist isn't called Beltram and is training 2 hours more than Winog, but 2 hours less than the warrior who is 20 years old.

The warrior training 18 hours a week is older than the one using the lance, but younger than Beltram.

The one training 24 hours a week is 2 years older than Gwennole, but 1 year younger than the sword fighter.

Alarig is the oldest; he trains 4 hours less than the club-fighter, but 2 hours more than the archer.

No quarter

Caesar's armies have begun to lay siege to free Gaul, and the ferocious warriors defending the territory of Pou-Niairisson, the deep heart of Celtic culture, are expecting the help of the gods. To receive this, they are making woven wicker cages in which they will put the Romans along with some straw, and burn as a form of offering.

The druid divides up the work according to ability. A first team has the task of making the largest cages, able to hold eight Romans; a second team makes cages that can hold four Romans, and a third team makes smaller cages to contain three Romans.

It takes 5 hours to weave the largest wicker cage, 3 hours for the next size down, and 2 and a half hours for the smallest.

If the union only allows work days of 12 hours, how much time will it take the Gauls of Pou-Niairisson to make enough wicker cages to prepare the sacrifice of 31 legionnaires to Toutatis and co.?

Solution p. 159.

Puzzle

Ca you reconstruct this Celtic figure?

Place pieces A, B, C, D, E and F into the squares numbered 1 to 6.   *Solution p. 132.*

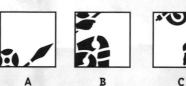

A   B   C

D   E   F

1	2
3	4
5	6

TREASURE

Five Celtic coins are hidden in this meadow, marked out in a grid, for which we have given you the plan and the following clues:

• There are no coins in the squares with numbers in them.
• The numbers in the squares indicate the number of adjacent squares containing a coin.
• There is only one coin per square.

Examples:

Solution p. 179.

for the table below, the possible solutions are:

 →

Complete the grid:

	2		
I		2	
3	3		I

32

Mouths to feed

Well may they have rubbed their bellies against the tall menhir while calling on Manawydan on nights of the full moon, but Owein and his wife have not had any children, and so it was with the greatest joy that the couple welcomed two little orphans, a brother and sister, that the druid was good enough to introduce them to.

But while this joy was shared by the children, they nevertheless did not want to be separated from the rest of their siblings.
— Are there lots of you then? Owein asked the little girl.
— I have as many brothers as sisters, replied Morwenna.
— I have twice as many sisters as brothers, her brother added.

How many boys and girls will the couple have to adopt?

Solution p. 153.

The long march of helix aspersa

Did the gods favour an attack before the full moon, or after the full moon? A red slug and a holy snail were set off from the same starting line, both attracted by a little barley beer spilled at the foot of a menhir some distance away. Ms Slug proceeded straight ahead, salivating with anticipation, her feelers pointed towards the aromatic goal, at a speed of 2 metres per hour. Mr Snail, for his part, having already partaken of the barley beer, moved at a steady speed of 5 metres an hour, but has moved in zigzags, so that our two gastropods end up arriving at the same time at the foot of the menhir. The attack will therefore take place during the full moon.

If the menhir is 2 metres from the starting line, what distance has the holy (and completely sloshed) snail covered?

Solution p. 153.

Change

A short lesson from the great druid Cathbad:

'I have two coins in my purse. The total value of the coins in my purse is equal to five times the value of my first coin and the difference between the two coins is 6.'

How much do the coins in his purse add up to?

First coin  =?

Second coin =?

Solution p. 139.

The fibula calculation

A merchant has laid out a beautiful woollen coat in an intense shade of red, a magnificent crimson, fastened with three fibulae. He declares that he wants 112 bronze coins for it to a warrior with a long red moustache, who protests: 'I've already got some fibulae, I only want the coat. You'll have to give me a discount, a good one too … Shall we say 60 then?'

There are strong protestations from the merchant, who quickly bundles the coat away into his big wooden chest:
'A coat like this costs a hundred coins more than the three fibulae!
This fellow wants to ruin me!'

How much does a fibula cost?

Solution p. 156.

Poems

Four young men are writing poems for their beloved. For each suitor, you have to work out who his heart's desire is and the number of poems he has written for her.

	4	5	7	9	Alastrine	Eirlys	Fiona	Sezaic
Laig								
Malou								
Quirec								
Ruadhagan								
Alastrine								
Eirlys								
Fiona								
Sezaic								

Clues:
Laig has written more poems than the man inspired by Sezaic, but less than the one inspired by Eirlys.

Quirec has written 5 poems. They were dedicated neither to Sezaic, nor Fiona.

Malou is in love with Eirlys.

Solution p. 148.

The courage of Enora

You need courage if you're a young woman, in order to travel upstream steering a currach!

It's on such a watercraft, made of hides sewn together and stretched over a wicker frame, that young Enora has left in search of her husband, Efflam, who, preferring the chastity of monastic life, has fled the conjugal home and put precisely 73 leagues between himself and his spouse.

So Enora rows, rows, rows …
She valiantly rows the whole day long, and travels up the river 5 leagues. But she has to sleep at night to restore her strength, and the currach, left to the current, systematically retreats 4 leagues downstream.

How many days will it take Enora to reach Efflam?

Solution p. 156.

The bard

The bard of this Celtic tribe sang from evening to morning.
He had songs for every occasion:

38 songs for festivals,
28 songs calling to eat,
38 songs announcing religious ceremonies.

Some of these songs were for special occasions:
14 were for festive meals,
10 were for religious banquets,
9 were for religious festivals.

2 songs could be sung on any occasion.

**How many different songs does this bard have in his
repertoire?**
Tip: start with the 2 songs that can be sung on any occasion.

Solution p. 177.

39

The age of Glúingel

After successfully negotiating the ninth break, beyond which they had for a long time been held at bay by the druids of Dé Danann by the conjuring up of a magical storm, the eight sons of Mile launch into an attack on the land of Ireland.

Three of the sons survived, the three sons who killed the three kings of Tuatha Dé Danann in hand-to-hand combat, and who Mile had named Eber Finn, Eremon and Amergin the bard, called Glúingel, meaning 'white knees'.

The eldest, Glúingel, which is to say Amergin, is eleven years older than the next youngest brother. Who in turn is eleven years older than his junior, Eber Finn. A useful detail: the eldest is double the age of the youngest.

How old is each of the brothers?

Solution p. 178.

Cairn

A burial chamber has been covered with stones, forming a cairn. Archaeologists are excavating the site, but don't want to destroy the inner walls of the chamber. They have discovered a sort of site plan, but it is in code. You have to help them work out the layout.

Colour in the walls of the grid, on the principle that the number in each square indicates how many sides of the square it is in are filled in. The wall plan will thus appear.

Solution p. 127.

0	I	0	2	I	0
0	2	2	2	I	I
2	2	2	I	2	2
I	I	2	2	2	I
0	2	I	I	2	I
I	2	0	I	I	0

Dice game

Laorans and Paskal are playing a game of dice. Seeing Paskal's two dice, Laorans, who still has one die to throw, declares:

'Whatever the value of my second die, I am sure to make at least three times your score.'

Why does he make this declaration?

Solution p. 135.

Embroidery

Work out what pattern Viviane is embroidering on her tunic.
We have given you the sequence of points to fill in (starting from
the left of each row and the top of each column): for example,
3 1 in a row means that, starting from the left of the row, there will
be 3 filled-in points in a row, then 1 filled-in point by itself. It's up
to you to work out, by cross-checking the rows and columns,
where they are …   *Solution p. 121.*

Example:

3 1

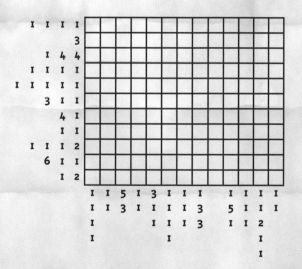

Origins

For these four men, work out what kind of house they live in and what land they come from.

	Thatch cottage	Log cabin	Stone house	Mud hut	Brittany	Scotland	Wales	Ireland
Egarec								
Hingrad								
Juvad								
Yaouen								
Brittany				
Scotland				
Wales				
Ireland				

Clues:

Egarec lives in the log cabin.
The man who lives in the stone house is Irish.
Hingrad is Welsh.
A Breton lives in the mud hut and he is not called Yaouen.

Solution p. 149.

Magic diamond

Bressan the soothsayer sets this little game for his pupils.
All of the lines and both diagonals of this magic diamond add up
to the same amount.

What is the smallest possible value of ᚻ, between X and XXV?

Solution p. 137.

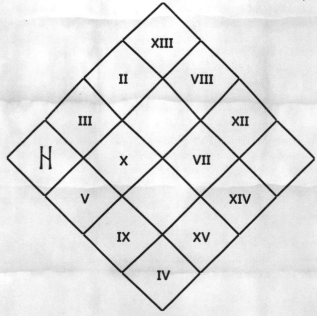

Chain reaction

The Santoni may well be a proud and feisty Celtic people in free or 'long-haired' Gaul, but they aren't known for splitting hairs. There are, however, situations where some advantage may be gained from looking before leaping.

A large rocky promontory lies along the sea front, bordered by a marshy zone opposite an island covered in pines and ferns, which is inhabited by savages who eat cuttlefish and snails, the Rhêtâs. The bank of one of the coves in this rocky promontory was hospitable enough to found a village there around a port, the village of the Rupelloux.

Periodically the Rhêtâs come and raid the Rupelloux's supplies, an improement on their usual diet. It's enough to make one tear one's hair out ... So the Rupelloux decide to block the entrance to their port with an enormous bronze chain, made from rings or links that are 2 feet across. Given the weight of each ring, 8 six-ring chains have been delivered by oxcart, and the oxen will also have the job of joining the 8 pieces together on site to make a great chain that can be stretched from one side of the entrance of their port to the other.

Given it takes a whole day to saw a link open, and a whole day to weld together an opened chain, how many days will it take the Rupelloux to make the chain in the shortest possible time?

Solution p. 160.

Puzzle

Can you reconstruct this Celtic figure?

Place pieces A, B, C, D, E and F into the squares numbered 1 to 6.   *Solution p. 133.*

A

B

C

D

E

F

1	2
3	4
5	6

Collection of animals

Place the missing pairs of animals into their correct place, assuming there's one of each of the five animals in each row, each column and each diagonal of the grid. One pair doesn't fit into the grid: which one?

5

6

7

8

I   **2**   **3**   **4**

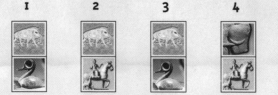

Solution p. 142.

48

Lawfully wedded

Given that nothing forbids an Armorican druid from marrying, and that conjugal relations in no way prevent him from carrying out his priestly functions, is there any major obstacle to a druid, married to a widow who is herself an Armorican Celt, remarrying the elder or younger sister of his widow?

Solution p. 160.

Written by the wind

*According to the Gauls
What's the difference
Between pea soup
And a little flatulence?*

Solution p. 161.

Magic diamond

Bressan the soothsayer sets this little game for his pupils.
All of the lines and both diagonals of this magic diamond add up
to the same amount.

What is the smallest possible value of Һ between X and XXV?

Solution p. 138.

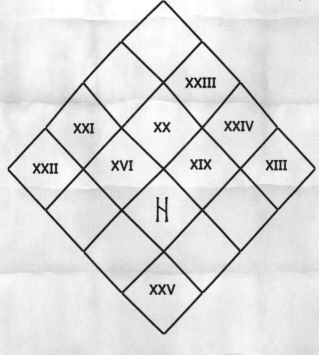

Magic square

Bressan the soothsayer sets this little game for his pupils.
Each row, column and corner-to-corner diagonal of this magic
square adds up to the same amount.

What is the value of ᚺ?

Solution p. 151.

			IV	I
		IV		III
	ᚺ		II	
III	IV			
II				

Cost of the menhir

The Bajocasses of a small village have all been pitching in funds to have a fine menhir erected on the hill that overlooks the surrounding countryside, and they break open the communal piggybank.

To have the menhir cut from a fantastic slab of pink sandstone, it cost them a fifth of their kitty.

To have the menhir transported, it cost them a fifth of what was left.

They still have 45 gold staters to erect the menhir, feast like pigs and calmly contemplate the repairs to the dolmen and village hall.

How much did they have in the piggybank?

Solution p. 161.

Puzzle

Ten pieces of a drawing of a Celtic interlacing have been found.
An interlacing can be reconstructed using eight of the pieces.

Which pieces are not needed?   *Solution p. 133.*

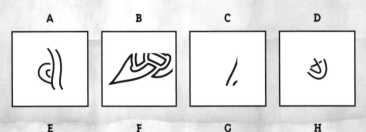

A   B   C   D

E   F   G   H

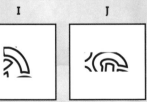

I   J

Change

A short lesson from the great druid Cathbad:

'I have two coins in my purse. The value of my first coin is equal to twice the value of the second or to the product of the second coin and the first.'

How much do the coins in Cathbad's purse add up to?

First coin =?

Second coin =?

Solution p. 140.

Bottoms up

The druid Cosmetix has sent young Herveline to get some
mare's milk to concoct a potion to treat a nasty case of eczema
afflicting the right buttock of the chief's wife. It's a bit of a trip,
a three-day walk.

Herveline fills up her goatskin, goblet by goblet. She starts on
the path back home with twelve goblets' worth of mare's milk,
or about one and a half litres. At mid-morning Herveline feels
the need to replenish herself: she pours a goblet of mare's milk,
drinks it and feels revitalised. She takes the precaution of filling
her goblet with water at the first spring she comes across and
pours the contents into her goatskin to make up for what she has
taken out for her own personal consumption. She does the same
thing at midday — to refresh herself, you understand — and the
same thing again at 5 p.m. — to restore herself. The next two days
see her repeat exactly the same pattern, and she arrives in sight of
her village completely revitalised, reinvigorated and restored, like
an ad for an organic Mare's Milk snake oil, with a delicious taste
reminiscent, would you believe, of coconut milk — in an era when
ads, which didn't yet exist, couldn't have referred to coconut
milk, which wasn't yet known … There's a lot that's fishy here.

**When she reaches the druid's place and hands over the
goatskin, approximately how many goblets' worth of mare's
milk is she is giving him, in your opinion?**

Solution p. 161.

A lot from a little

— No doubt this new riddle will not put up too much of a fight,
apprentice druid, easy as it is. But I'm sure you'll have the
manners to wait a little before giving your response, out of respect
for your master and initiator; you'll be looking to take your time
and have enough tact to seem like you're struggling a bit — you
can't be congratulated too much for your consideration, O'Gorilh!

Here is the riddle:

> On the one hand
> The more you take away from me
> The bigger I'll become
> On the other
> I'll be quite fulfilled
> If you give it all back

What on earth could it be?

Solution p. 162.

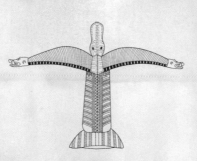

Embroidery

Work out what pattern Viviane is embroidering on her tunic.
We have given you the sequence of points to fill in (starting from
the left of each row and the top of each column): for example,
3 1 in a row means that, starting from the left of the row, there will
be 3 filled-in points in a row, then 1 filled-in point by itself. It's up
to you to work out, by cross-checking the rows and columns,
where they are …   *Solution p. 122.*
Example:

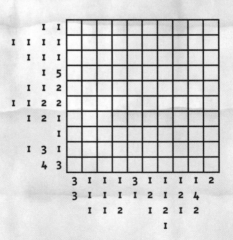

Good accounts make good friends ...

Three farmers are going to sell their potatoes at the market.

The produce of the first farmer is equal to a quarter of the total produce.
The produce of the second farmer is 5 kilograms of potatoes.
The produce of the third farmer equals the sum of the produce of the two others.

The put all their produce together.

How many kilograms of potatoes do they have to sell?

Solution p. 177.

Fairs

Four young women have to go to the great spring fair in the nearest town. Work out which town each of them goes to and how much time she spends there.

	Alesia	Burdigala	Juliomagus	Lutetia	6 days	8 days	10 days	12 days
Benedig								
Kristell								
Rhiannon								
Ysolda								
6 days								
8 days								
10 days								
12 days								

Clues:
Kristell's stay lasts 4 days more than that of the young woman who goes to Lutetia and whose name is not Ysolda.

The one who goes to Burdigala is not called Kristell and she stays longer than Benedig.

Rhiannon stays in Juliomagus 2 days longer than the one who goes to Alesia. She stays there longer than the one whose trip lasts 8 days.

Solution p.149.

Druids

Three peasants go to see the druids for their digestive troubles.
The druid takes out his flask of stomach potion and gives:

a third of the potion to the first,
half to the second,
half the amount given to the first to the last peasant.

How much potion is there left in the flask?

Solution p. 178.

Druid specialties

In this Celtic tribe, all of the druids had a specialty:

100 druids taught at least music,
60 druids taught at least history,
40 druids taught at least poetry,

40 taught at least music and history,
15 taught at least poetry and history,
35 taught at least poetry and music,

Ten taught all 3 subjects.

How many druids were there in this tribe?

Tip: start with the 10 druids who teach all 3 subjects.

Solution p.178.

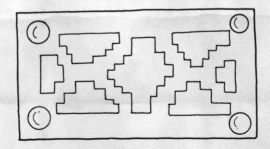

Collection of jewellery

Place the missing jewellery into the correct places, if there's one of each of the five types of jewellery in each row, each column, and each diagonal of the grid. One pair doesn't fit into the grid: which one?

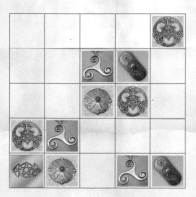

5

6

7

8

I

2

3

4

Solution p. 143.

The inseparables

King Eochaid Feidlech has three sons known as the Trí Finn Emna, 'the three fair inseparable ones': Bres, Nár and Lothar.
The three fair inseparables have to go and visit their sister Clothru, who has a surprise in store for them, and who lives 12 leagues away. But the three sons of the king have to share between them an old nag who goes at 10 leagues an hour and can only carry two riders at a time.
On foot, the fair inseparables can only hobble along at a speed of 2 leagues an hour.

What should they do so that all three arrive at Clothru in the shortest possible amount of time? *Solution p. 162.*

Procession of bugs

Gandalf regarded with amazement three bugs running along in single file on his magic wand. Three tiny little bugs. His amazement was not due to the presence of the insects, because the light that shone out the end of the wand explained well enough why they might be attracted there. What perplexed him deeply was that he heard them, clearly and distinctly, speak:

'Help! Help! Help! I'm being followed by a green thing with legs and antennae!' said the first one in a tiny little voice.
'Help! Help! Help! I'm being followed by a green thing with legs and antennae!' cried the second one in a tiny little voice.
'Help! Help! Help! I'm being followed by a green thing with legs and antennae!' cried the third one in a tiny little voice.
'And yet, what they say is true ...' murmured Gandalf.

How do you explain this?
Solution p. 163.

Puzzle

Can you reconstruct this Celtic figure?

Place pieces A, B, C, D, E and F into the squares numbered 1 to 6. *Solution p. 134.*

A

B

C

D

E

F

1	2
3	4
5	6

TREASURE

Seven Celtic coins 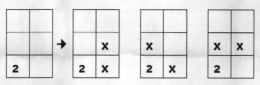 are hidden in this meadow, marked out in a grid, for which we have given you the plan and the following clues:

• There are no coins in the squares with numbers in them.
• The numbers in the squares indicate the number of adjacent squares containing a coin.
• There is only one coin per square.

Examples:

Solution p. 179.

for the table below, the possible solutions are:

2	

→

	X
2	X

X	
2	X

X	X
2	

Complete the grid

		2		I
	2	3		
2				2
				2
2		2	I	I

Myrdhin's precious stones

Myrdhin, the official druid and sorcerer of his state, is counting the gold staters he has stored up in his purse: 130 staters, not one more, not one less. With this considerable sum, which he plans to spend in full, he will be able to procure the precious and semi-precious stones he needs to make some magic potions for which he holds the secret. And it's a very expensive business.

At these kinds of prices you don't get change, and in any case the lapidary only sets his prices in round figures: a tourmaline costs one stater, a topaz two staters, a cordierite three, a citrine four, an amethyst five, an aquamarine six, a ruby seven, a sapphire eight, an emerald nine and a diamond ten.

Since he is as superstitious a man as he is Pythagorean, and attaches the greatest importance to numbers, Myrdhin buys as many stones of the same sort as each stone costs in staters: if he decides to buy an emerald, which costs nine staters, he has to buy nine of them!

But going on that method, his choice is in fact quite limited: which stones will he bring back in his pouch?

Solution p. 163.

By Belenus!

A drakkar lost at the threshold of Armorica and driven by a violent northerly wind is dashed to pieces against the sacred island of Tombelaine. A terrible disaster, a terrible shipwreck in a wild and icy sea that swallows down the Vikings and throws them back up on the shore at the mercy of the breakers! Soon the corpses are beyond number ...

This land is, however, a sacred land, and there's no question of it harbouring the bodies of hostile strangers for any length of time. Where, then, can the survivors be buried, given that the island, which is substantially composed of granite, is not really suited to the act of burial?

The question at hand is even more pressing since Mont Tombelaine, the resting place of Belenus, the sun god and god of the dead, is a border zone between two territories whose chiefs aren't on the friendliest terms with one another: the territory of the Ferocious Gwenegan to the east, and to the west the domain of Heneg the Bloody. Heneg, however, is the half-brother of Gwenegan's wife.

By Belenus, then, where?   *Solution p. 163.*

Dice game

Laorans and Paskal are playing a game of dice. Seeing Paskal's two dice, Laorans, who still has one die to throw, declares:

'If the value of my second die is triple the value of my first die, I will have quadrupled your score.'

What does he mean?

Solution p. 135.

Embroidery

Work out what pattern Viviane is embroidering on her tunic.
We have given you the sequence of points to fill in (starting from
the left of each row and the top of each column): for example,
3 1 in a row means that, starting from the left of the row, there will
be 3 filled-in points in a row, then 1 filled-in point by itself. It's up
to you to work out, by cross-checking the rows and columns,
where they are …   *Solution p.123.*

Example:

3 1

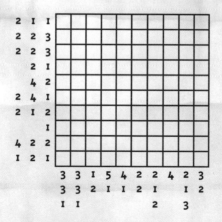

To each their own

A forgotten version of the Lebor Gabála Érenn (the Book of the Taking of Ireland) portrays on the eve of the third conquest, as a sort of parenthesis in the epic, a moment of peace and open camaraderie shared between the heros, the five sons of Dela.

Gann, Sengann, Sláine, Genann and Rudraige take a little time out with their wives, who are, from the youngest to the eldest: Ann, Maggy, Peggy, Raymonde and Mauricette.

a) Sláine's wife gathers sweet williams with Raymonde's husband.
b) Peggy and her husband, Genann, go fishing for mussels.
c) Sengann and Ann romp in the hay.
d) Rudraige and Mauricette catch butterflies.
e) Ann is not married to Rudraige.

Who is Sengann's wife?

Solution p. 163.

TREASURE

Eight Celtic coins 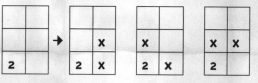 are hidden in this meadow, marked out in a grid, for which we have given you the plan and the following clues:

• There are no coins in the squares with numbers in them.
• The numbers in the squares indicate the number of adjacent squares containing a coin.
• There is only one coin per square.

Examples:

for the table below, the possible solutions are:

2	

→

	x
2	x

x	
2	x

x	x
2	

Complete the grid

Solution p. 179.

1			2	
	3		3	
2		4		2
	3		3	
		3		

Rearing chickens

— Before you learn to count the lunar months, young O'Gorilh, before you can predict the position of the stars at the time of the winter solstice, you will learn to count on your fingers, that will already be something.

See these chickens in these cages. There are as many cages as you have hands, and as many chickens as you have fingers. You can leave your nose alone. It takes three weeks for my chickens to hatch 23 eggs.

Imagine, young O'Gorilh, that I buy a third cage, and I put in it as many chickens as you have toes on your left foot.

How much time will it take the chickens in my cages to hatch 23 eggs?

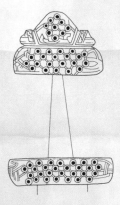

Solution p. 165.

Topless priestess

Picture a hellish fire beneath a gigantic cauldron, scalding steam filling the room, suffocating heat. The druid Mac O'Nith, a Briton from the Atrebates tribe, is bustling around the cauldron, grumbling: he is missing two leaves of pennyroyal, a large sieve and a wooden spoon.

'By Toutatis', he says to the priestess Fainne, who works as his assistant, 'you have all those things at your place, go quickly and fetch them!'
'But I'm only wearing a skirt and nothing else!' protests the priestess.
'Hurry up! It's urgent!'
'But I live 2 leagues away and in 5 minutes it's going to rain like a dragon taking a leak!'
'Get a move on!'

Fainne runs off, arrives home, gathers the three items and, without taking the time to pick up a coat, umbrella or anything of the sort, retraces her steps going back the other way ... under a deluge of rain which buckets down on the countryside almost as soon as she steps outside her house.

And yet when she returns, quite breathless, to Mac O'Nith's place and hands him the three items he asks for, not a hair on her head is wet ...

How on earth could she have managed this?

Solution p. 164.

hot potato

— Dust off your King Lears, O'Gorilh my friend, and heed my words closely. Here is today's riddle:

> *The one who makes it doesn't want it*
> *The one who buys it doesn't use it*
> *The one who uses it cannot see it*

What on earth could it be?

Solution p. 165.

Cairn

The burial chamber has been covered with stones, forming a cairn. The archaeologists excavating the site don't want to destroy the inner walls of the chamber. They have found a sort of map of the site, but it is coded. You have to help them discover the key.

Fill in the divisions of this grid, following the principle that the number in each box indicates the number of filled-in borders around it. You will thus make the wall plan appear.

2	2	1	2	1	1
2	3	3	3	0	0
1	1	3	2	2	2
2	2	2	0	2	2
1	2	1	1	1	1
0	2	1	1	1	1

Solution p. 128.

Pantheon

Which Celtic divinity is hidden behind these clues?

I am the most important divinity in the Celtic pantheon.

I am mother, sister, wife.

I am the goddess of both the arts and of war.

I am the equivalent of the Roman goddess Minerva.

Solution p. 141.

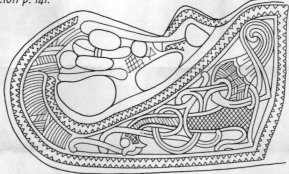

Bog off!

A frog is the happy owner of a pond in which a waterlily pad has just opened up, and the frog rubs her hands together with satisfaction because it will serve as a fine trampoline for splish-splashing about in the early morning.

All well and good, but here's the thing: the lily pad makes baby pads and each day the waterlily plant doubles in surface area, so that at the end of 50 days the pond is completely covered and if the frog still wants to show off her breaststroke to the local men frogs, she'd better pack her bags.

Not far away, she finds a second pond that's completely identical in size to the previous one, and sets down her suitcases and derrière on two lily pads that are completely identical to the first one, and each day they'll double in surface area, and pretty soon she'll have to pick herself up once again and go splish-splash elsewhere ... These pond problems are bogging her down — it's no life for a frog.

How many days does she have left, in fact?   *Solution p. 165.*

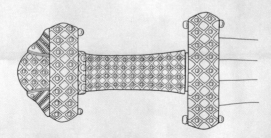

Collection of heads

Place the missing pairs of heads into their correct place, assuming there's one of each of the five heads in each row, each column and each diagonal of the grid. One pair doesn't fit into the grid: which one?

5

6

7

8

1   **2**   **3**   **4**

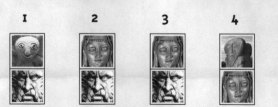

Solution p. 144.

Calcium for the agriculturist

Joseph MacBowen is a farmer and proud to be one. He tends his land and owns three sickles in different sizes — one for the barley, one for the oats and the third for the wheat — and has earned himself a reputation as a specialist in their use. He has, in addition, a small kitchen garden in front of his thatched cottage. He leads a healthy life, is a member of the anti-barley beer brigade, and to keep himself in shape, every evening after his frugal meal he drinks a bowl of milk on his doorstep, watching the sun set and listening to his lentils grow.

This farmer has no cows. And, in fact, even if he wanted to keep them, he couldn't: contact with cows gives him a terrible allergic reaction, on which the druid's potions have had no effect.

He doesn't buy milk. He doesn't borrow it, steal it and no one gives it to him. Nevertheless, every evening, after his grain porridge, down the hatch, a bowl of milk …

Is Joseph MacBowen a farmer, or a magician?

Solution. 165.

Cairn

The burial chamber has been covered with stones, forming a cairn. The archaeologists excavating the site don't want to destroy the inner walls of the chamber. They have found a sort of map of the site, but it is coded. You have to help them discover the key.

Fill in the divisions of this grid, following the principle that the number in each box indicates the number of filled-in borders around it. You will thus make the wall plan appear.

Solution p. 129.

I	O	2	I	2	I
2	2	2	O	I	O
O	2	I	2	2	2
I	2	2	3	2	2
I	I	I	2	I	I
I	2	I	2	I	I

In moderation

When the atmosphere heats up at the Celtic Hotel, you can always find an innocent, a sucker, an out-of-towner who's running off at the mouth and not from round here who you can put the following drinking problem to: it's their shout for the next round of barley beer if they can't solve it.

Lined up along the sticky table, starting from the left, are four skulls filled with a fermented beverage, followed by four empty skulls. The challenge consists in obtaining a strictly alternating row of full skulls and empty skulls, but by only touching two skulls and no more.
If that's not moderation …

Put yourself in the place of the sucker. Nothing personal, of course.

Solution p. 165.

The soft sound of the egg

'I'm very, very hungry and I must leave straightaway, I'll have to take something with me to eat!' says Fanch, his swag thrown over his shoulder.
'I don't have time to put anything together.' Fanchann shoots back, 'I'm off to milk the cows. I hard-boiled an egg last night, you can take that. A hard-boiled egg fills you up nicely.'

Fanch opens the pantry door and sees not one but six eggs. He takes one at random and taps it on the table to peel it: curses! Terrible is the soft sound of an egg you thought was hard, which cracks in the most unfortunate way, spilling its precious contents which dribble through your fingers, stick to the table and run down irrevocably to the beaten-earth floor: it's a raw egg. Fanchann will be happy!

Fanch takes the five remaining eggs, places them on the table and looks them in the eyes, saying to himself: I absolutely have to go, which one should I take?

The first one is almost pink, the second one is white, the third borders on brown, the fourth is a little yellow, and the fifth displays pretty shades of mauve.

'Ah!' he says. 'I've got it, I know now!'

And what does our friend Fanch know?
Solution p. 166.

The five Bituriges

— Listen to your old druid friend closely, young O'Gorilh, and reflect.

Five Celts, who belong to a tribe of Bituriges, are shedding hot tears and directing towards the heavens a slow and dirge-like chanting that would make a Brittany spaniel whimper.

There's no drunkenness in this story, oh apprentice druid, no boozing or carousing, our five Celts are quite simply sad, deathly sad. Which is understandable, since their father, mother and brother are being buried, having been laid low by Kerfinn-Jakobsen disease.

It's a first-class burial. A small terracotta statue of the mother goddess Dé Danann has been placed in the common grave. A few stone slabs, a few shovelfuls of earth: their tears are understandable given that the members of the family can now be counted on one hand, and henceforth these Celts have no brother.

Really, no brother?
Are they deranged with grief,
O'Gorilh? Or have the Bituriges
been bingeing after all?

Solution p. 166.

Memory gap

The druid Mac Silere is sitting on his money chest, holding his right jaw, rather distressed. He has just been mugged; there's just no respect these days.

A fake bard in a false beard tried to force the lid of the money chest with a crowbar.
Fortunately, the druid came along in time to tell him that the crowbar would be of no use, as the chest was protected by a secret combination mechanism and was as well clad in iron as a two-year-old pig is in lard.
Unfortunately, he learned — at his jaw's expense — a use for the crossbar he hadn't thought of.
Fortunately, the robber left without making any further demands on his pockets.
Unfortunately, the blow the druid received has made him forget the four-figure combination that will let him get into the chest, and he needs to pay his housekeeper.
Fortunately, he remembers that the sum of the four figures is equal to the number of digits on a one-legged man, that the last figure is twice the value of the first and that the second is the third of the third figure.

What is the code?

Solution p. 166.

Cairn

The burial chamber has been covered with stones, forming a cairn. The archaeologists excavating the site don't want to destroy the inner walls of the chamber. They have found a sort of map of the site, but it is coded. You have to help them discover the key.

Fill in the divisions of this grid, following the principle that the number in each box indicates the number of filled-in borders around it. You will thus make the wall plan appear.

Solution p. 130.

I	2	3	2	0	I
2	2	3	3	I	2
2	3	2	3	3	I
2	3	2	3	3	2
2	3	3	3	2	2
I	I	I	2	2	I

Embroidery

Work out what pattern Viviane is embroidering on her tunic.
We have given you the sequence of points to fill in (starting from
the left of each row and the top of each column): for example,
3 1 in a row means that, starting from the left of the row, there will
be 3 filled-in points in a row, then 1 filled-in point by itself. It's
up to you to work out, by cross-checking the rows and columns,
where they are …
Solution p. 124.

Example:

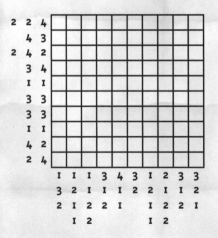

Shilly-shallying

Following a division of labour that has hardly progressed since Neanderthal man left his cave to Homo Sapiens and whoever he shared his bathroom with, two fathers and two sons were sitting at the dinner table while Pegeen, a housewife, busied herself with the cooking.

'By Danann, you are a pearl, Pegeen!' exclaimed one of them as she placed a steaming acorn pie on the table.
'Hurry up and eat it and get out from under my feet, I have to clean the house before going out to milk the cows, feed the chickens, sort the lentils, iron your breeches, weed the peas, fetch some water, do the ...'
'This is no time for your shilly-shallying! the other continued. We need help to shift the menhir. Just this once you'll eat a piece with us to garner a little strength!'

He takes out his seax and in two swipes — whack! thwack! — he cuts the pie into four equal pieces.

He's counted right, hasn't he?
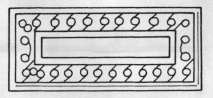

Solution p. 166.

Pantheon

Which Celtic divinity is hidden behind these clues?

I am one of the most important gods in the Gallic pantheon.

I am the god of thunder and lightning.

I am often accompanied by a horse, eagle or snake.

I am the equivalent of the Roman god Jupiter.

Solution p. 141.

Collection of objects

Place the missing pairs of Celtic objects correctly into the grid, assuming there's one of each of the 5 objects in each row, each column and each diagonal of the grid. One pair doesn't fit into the grid: which one?

5

6

7

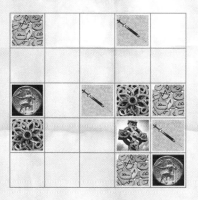

8

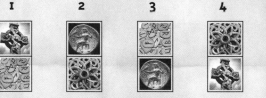

I   **2**   **3**   **4**

Solution p. 145.

No hands,
no abacus

Using its beak, the crow is going to move one, and only one, of these twigs which have fallen from the sacred willow tree, so that it spells out — until the next gust of wind — a message of truth. And all that without an abacus.

How?

II-IV=V

Solution p. 167.

Head and Feet

— Do you realise, apprentice druid, what extraordinary labour and skills are required to arrange the menhirs in a cromlech like that! It's not just a matter of muscles, it's brains as well: everything has been calculated — the height of the stones, their distance in relation to the others in each concentric circle, the spacing of the circles in relation to each other, the orientation of the whole group in relation to the solstice, the temperature of the barley beer and the age of the captain.

The day has come for you to demonstrate your know-how in the area of arithmetic: lets see if you can work out a modest problem. It's one that has the whiff of the farmyard about it — we will see afterwards if you are worthy of rising to more spiritual heights.

Our neighbour MacBowen keeps pigs and laying hens in his yard. If he can count 9 heads and 32 feet in total, how many chickens does MacBowen have, and how many pigs?

Solution p. 167.

Pantheon

Which Celtic divinity is hidden behind these clues?

*I am a goddess worshipped in Gaul,
but also in Wales under the name Rhiannon or in
Ireland under the name Macha.*

*Associated with the horse,
I am the goddess of the military aristocracy.*

*My worship spread throughout a considerable
portion of Europe and even as far as Rome where a
temple was erected in my honour.*

I am the goddess of fertility.

Solution p. 141.

Embroidery

Work out what pattern Viviane is embroidering on her tunic.
We have given you the sequence of points to fill in (starting from
the left of each row and the top of each column): for example,
3 1 in a row means that, starting from the left of the row, there will
be 3 filled-in points in a row, then 1 filled-in point by itself. It's up
to you to work out, by cross-checking the rows and columns,
where they are...   *Solution p. 125.*

Example:

3 1

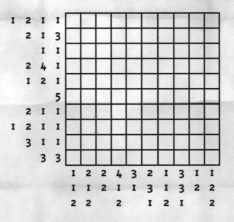

Well spotted, blind fellow!

The setting of Myrdhin's dream was an icy and sinister cave at the furthest reaches of the known world, in a country where no Celtic hand had ever set foot. In the middle of the cave, three figures were tied to three posts so that they faced each other. There was a monocule, a cynocephalus who was blind in one eye, and a completely blind blemmye.

The monocule, as his name suggests, had just one eye, in the middle of his forehead; the cynocephalus had given his fellow creatures so much of the evil eye he only had sight left in his left one; and the blemmye, whose face — as is the case with all blemmyes — was located in the middle of his torso, had ended up putting his eyes out from beating his chest.

Myrdhin had a role in his own dream: he saw himself with a bag slung across his shoulder, which contained four extremely pretty crowns of holly.

'Of these four crowns' he explained to the three creatures tied to the posts, 'one crown and one crown only has red berries. I am going to pass behind each of you and place a crown on your head. The first one who can tell me if he is wearing a green crown or a red and green crown will be set free.'

As he said, so he did: our three prisoners found themselves topped with a leafy crown.

Five minutes later, the monocule still hadn't said anything.

Ten minutes passed, the cynocephalus still seemed to be mute.

Then the blemmye, as blind as he was, cried out: 'I'm free!'

Why?

Solution p. 168.

Utopia?

Myrdhin still didn't manage to wake up, and his strange dream continued ...

'Come to my place,' said the blemmye whom he had freed, 'you'll see, it's nice: it only has one wall and everything faces due south!'

How do you, who are not blind, see this situation?

Solution p. 169.

Pantheon

Which Celtic divinity is hidden behind these clues?

I am the supreme god of Celtic mythology.

Often represented as a crow, I am worshipped under the same name among all the Celtic peoples.

I am the master of beauty and thought.

My name is associated with the city of Lyon.

Solution p. 141.

Uchronia?

There is a very special place, a very quiet place and also in a certain way full of noise and fury, a place that you usually move through using your hands, a place where you might use your hands to move through it, but you don't walk upside down; a place, I say, a strange place where, imagine this, Thursday comes before Wednesday.

Where is this place?

Solution p. 169.

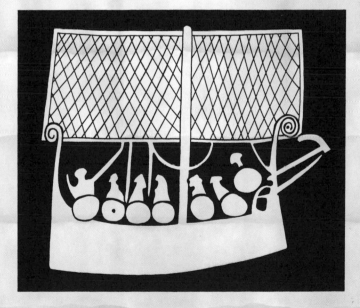

Breton removalists

The job is to move a small, private dolmen made up of two stone pillars supporting a table stone. Total weight: 300 tonnes. One of the pillars, the smallest one, weighs a quarter of the combined weight of the two other pieces, and the table stone, which is the heaviest of the three, weighs 20 tonnes less than the two others combined.

How much does each element of the dolmen weigh?

Solution p. 169.

Dice game

Laorans and Paskal are playing a game of dice. Laorans has thrown his two dice three times and Paskal twice.
Paskal takes up just one of his dice for his last throw:
'If I throw a 4, I will have doubled your score. But if I throw a 1, we will have a tie.'

What is the value of the die that Paskal doesn't throw again?

Solution p. 136.

101

The spendthrift druid

With nimble fingers, the druid Mac Rodach'Tyl takes from the
royal treasure as many precious stones as he thinks necessary and,
on the order of the new King of Ireland, goes to fetch the five
talismans that are to ensure the prosperity of the whole tribe.

He thus comes back laden with the Stone of Fál, the Spear of Lugh,
the Sword of Núadu, the Cauldron of the Dagda, and the Braces of
William, venerable objects that he also happened to buy in that
order. He thus returns laden, but also relieved of all his precious
stones, down to the last one.

'It's incredible' the king said to him, 'I was under the impression
that I let you take, as a precaution, much more than would be
needed! Could any have been stolen from you in some inn, did
you hand some over to some creature, could you have lost some?
How many did you, in fact, use?'
'No idea … But I remember that with each purchase, each talisman
cost me half of what was in my purse, plus five stones.'
'Such a spendthrift, that one! Just as well I know how to count!'
the king sighed.

**How many precious stones did the druid take from the royal
treasure?**

Solution p. 170.

Stuff and nonsense

Konan and Konogan are twin brothers. But the fairy who hovered over their cradle blessed them very unequally in the area of neurones and muscle.

They are responsible, taking turns, for preparing the haggis — which is to say, a stuffed sheep's stomach — for all the inhabitants of their small village, on the occasion of the great festival of the sun and the harvests, Lughnasadh. It's just not Lughnasadh without a communal feast of stuffed sheep's stomach, while flaming hay bales tumble down the Hibernian hills under the delighted eye of the goddess Tailtiu!

However, while Konan takes six hours to chop up the haggis stuffing for Lughnasadh, Konogan, for his part, takes three.

If this year they join forces and work together to prepare the stuffed sheep's stomach for the communal feast, how much time will it take them?

Solution p. 171.

Ounces

Wearing their ceremonial white sagums, the 50 initiates are completing a circle of the cromlech singing a hymn to the god Lugh. Among these white-robed initiates are 31 bards. Since the training of these bards consists of learning to play the lyre, they have been invited to bring their instruments to produce the accompaniment, just as was written in their homework books.

But the chief druid, who has the eyes and ears of the chief inspector, can clearly see that the instructions have not been religiously observed: among the 50 howling halfwits going round the cromlech, he counts 30 who don't have a lyre.

How many bards haven't brought their instrument?

Solution p. 171.

Collection of helmets

Place the missing pairs of helmets in their correct place, assuming there's one of each of the five helmets in each row, each column and each diagonal of the grid. One pair doesn't fit into the grid: which one?

5

6

7

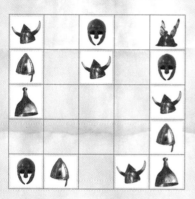

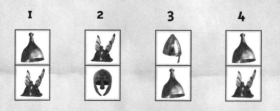

I **2** **3** **4**

Solution p. 146.

Daddy's girl

A druid buys four fibulae for his daughters: Pim, Pam, Poum and Zézette.

The fibulae he gives to Pim, Pam and Poum cost him 39 bronze coins.
The fibulae he gives to Pim, Pam and Zézette cost him 38 bronze coins.
The fibulae he gives to Pim, Poum and Zézette cost him 28 bronze coins.
The fibulae he gives to Pam, Poum and Zézette cost him 27 bronze coins.

If affection can be measured in cash, which daughter is the druid's favourite, and how much did her fibula cost?

Solution p. 172.

Pantheon

Which Celtic divinity is hidden behind these clues?

I am a totemic god.

Half-god, half-deer,
I am called on for everything that involves nature.

I oversee the transition between the world of the
living and the world of the dead.

Solution p. 141.

The hydra of Loch Breux

A valiant Pict warrior, all tattooed in blue, is dawdling along a lake in his native Scotland when suddenly a horrifying monster springs up, made of several serpents arching out in all directions from a single hideous body mounted on two ridiculous paws. The Pict's blood runs cold, his pulse starts racing, and with a swipe of his sword he slices off the bodies of half the serpents, cuts another of the serpents in half, and goes on his way.

Then along comes another Pict, all tattooed in blue, who gets the same nasty surprise, his pulse starts racing, and he does the same thing, then goes on his way.

A third Pict comes along, same story.

The monster, now with only three serpents, manages to drag itself to the riverbank and disappears into the waters of the lake.

How many serpent heads are squirming on the ground, whimpering?

Solution p. 172.

Amuse-gueules

The druids of Armorica arrive in the forest of Brocéliande for their major yearly gathering, and start to climb the ridge that looks over the Val Sans Retour, towards the Hotié de Viviane. Four of them find themselves together when they take a break: one belongs to the Osismii tribe, the other is Bajocasse, the third is one of the Lexovii tribe and the fourth is Veneti.

They show each other the gourds of mead and nuggets of honey-marinated boar they have brought to share when aperitif time comes following the sun worship ceremony, and they introduce themselves: their names are Edern, Dagon, Fezig and Gaston. Dagon has brought fewer nuggets than Edern, and Gaston has 23 more than Fezig.

The druid who has been delegated by the Osismii has brought twice as many boar nuggets as the Bajocasse druid, who has twice as many as the Veneti; as for this latter druid, he has twice outright the amount of the Lexovii druid.

The question everyone is asking themselves is: where's Dagon from, then?

Solution p. 173.

Pantheon

Which Celtic divinity is hidden behind these clues?

I am a warrior god.

My name means 'protector of the tribe'.

I am called on as a divine protector of the community.

My Roman equivalent is Mars.

Solution p. 141.

Double paradox

— Examine this essential truth carefully, young O'Gorilh, which your old druid is offering for your young mind to ruminate on:

The more there is of me, the less you see of me

What on earth could it be?

There are at least two answers that could solve the paradox ... so it's no use putting on that helpless and put-upon expression, O'Gorilh!

Solution p. 173.

Featherweight

— See this menhir split in two by lightning, whose top part now lies on the ground like a decapitated head: but it still holds four-sevenths of its weight up against the sky! Understand, young O'Gorilh, that this menhir, when it was whole, weighed 150 tonnes more than the part that lies on the ground.
Which you will now tidy up, it makes such a mess ...

But before you do that, answer this question:
How much did the menhir weigh? *Solution p. 173.*

Balls!

One day when the barley beer had been spiked with a little too much calvados, the soule team of a small Lexovii village called three Viducassii lingering at the Celtic Hotel a few choice names elaborating on the 'ass' theme, things came to blows and, to cut a long story short, now it's war.

The Viducassii, who are absolutely livid, have lots of balls, in every sense of the word: in effect their druid, who has brought back a few exotic recipes from his study trips abroad, has made 200 fire balls using a natural form of naphtha supplied to him by a colleague from the Arverni tribe. Sparks will really fly.

A quarter of the warriors have left for battle with a ball in each hand. The rest have taken just one each, with the exception of the last five, who were able to take five each.

How many men make up the Viducassii army?

Solution p. 174.

A bed of menhirs

— See these nine menhirs, young O'Gorilh? Your task today will be to line them up in such a way that a delighted eye can contemplate 10 rows of three menhirs, a little like graceful flowers ready to bloom in a well-maintained garden bed.

Don't go giving yourself a back sprain for nothing, start by drawing a sketch on the sand (what a numbskull this one is …)!

Solution p. 175.

Get your goat

Old Parann O'Iach' is a fusspot of the worst kind: Sir cannot bear odd numbers.

He has bought six goats in the neighbouring village, and needs his grandson to build them not one but four pens in the small field that adjoins his kitchen garden.

Things would be simple if the old man hadn't decided, in addition, that his new pets have to be distributed among the four pens so that none of the pens is empty and all contain an even number of goats.

How can his grandson avoid vexing Grandpa O'Iach'?

Solution p. 175.

Slap happy

The pig bladder that each team will be trying to get a hold of out on the village square has been filled with sand: it's the big Saturday-night soule match and there's going to be blood and guts, sporting spirit, manliness and black eyes — great fun.

The members of the yellow-breeches team gather to one side to exchange a few final technical tips and encouraging words. To rev themselves up, they all let out a battle cry then each one slaps his hand against the palm of the other team members. Just one slap — it's not like they're little girls, I suppose you want to give them a skipping rope as well?

The bard Hilegavir O'Guindo, who has a very fine sense of hearing, counts 78 distinct slaps, in the time it takes to wish them a 'Gudh baigh, faire welle!' meaning, in proto-Irish, the most Celtic message of all: 'We'll show'em!'

How many players are there in the team?

Solution p. 176.

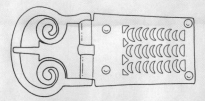

Fair share

Three Irish bards, Padraig, Quennegan and Reamann, have spent the day providing the entertainment at the Beltane festival, and now that evening has come, they have come together to continue the festivities in private and in honour of the horned god.

Padraig has brought 1.2 litres of a fermented beverage smelling of peat and iodine, Quennegan has come with 1.8 litres of a fermented beverage smelling of peat and iodine, and Reamann, the worthy descendant of Con Mhac ('son of dog', in Gaelic), says that the shops in his faraway Conmaícne Mara (Connemara, the land of the sons of dog) were shut.

Showing great benevolence towards the third world of their native Ireland, the two bards — not dogs — share the beverage three ways and each of them, in a series of 100 ml shots, ends up imbibing a third of the fermented liquid (hic!).

Reamann, who has a sense of fairness despite being as drunk as a North Germanian troll, rummages in the pockets of his breeches and pulls together 30 bronze coins that he intends to divide fairly between his two work colleagues to reimburse them for their expense.

You yourself reader — who perhaps combines a sense of fairness with one of sobriety and who thus, no doubt, has a clearer perception of the situation — how would you divide up the 30 pieces between Padraig and Quennegan?

Solution p. 176.

Solutions

Embroidery

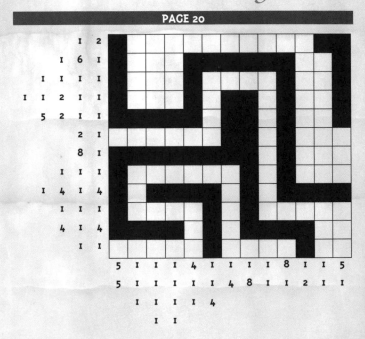

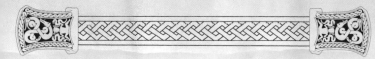

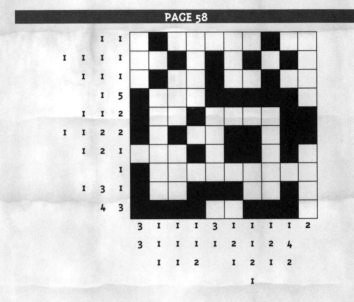

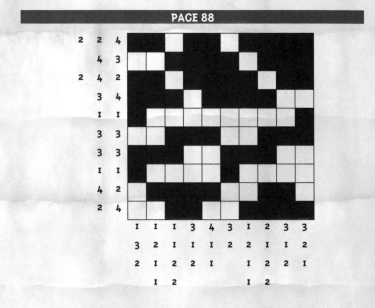

124

Cairn

0	0	2	1	2	1
2	2	2	1	2	1
1	1	1	2	1	1
2	2	1	2	1	1
1	2	2	0	2	2
0	1	1	0	1	0

PAGE 41

O	I	O	2	I	O
O	2	2	2	I	I
2	2	2	I	2	2
I	I	2	2	2	I
O	2	I	I	2	I
I	2	O	I	I	O

2	2	1	2	1	1
2	3	3	3	0	0
1	1	3	2	2	2
2	2	2	0	2	2
1	2	1	1	1	1
0	2	1	1	1	1

I	O	2	I	2	I
2	2	2	O	I	O
O	2	I	2	2	2
I	2	2	3	2	2
I	I	I	2	I	I
I	2	I	2	I	I

I	2	3	2	0	I
2	2	3	3	I	2
2	3	2	3	3	I
2	3	2	3	3	2
2	3	3	3	2	2
I	I	I	2	2	I

Caesar sabotaged

Solution

Caesar had every reason to suppose that Gaul was pacified. But when Crassus, needing grain to provide for his troops, sent out emissaries amongst the neighbouring Celtic states to demand a contribution, the Veneti revolted. They imprisoned the Roman envoys. It has to be said that this state was by far the most powerful on the whole sea coast. They had a very great number of ships, which they used to communicate with Britain; they surpassed other peoples in their knowledge and experience of navigation; and as controllers of the few ports scattered along that stormy and open sea, they extracted tributes from all who sailed in that region. They thus gave their neighbours the signal to revolt. They agreed to stand up to the Romans and act jointly. A very proud people, they chose to continue in that liberty which they had received from their ancestors rather than endure slavery under the invaders. But Caesar could not accept this and prepared to wage war.

Based on Julius Caesar's *Commentaries on the Gallic War*.

Puzzles

Solution
D, F and H
aren't needed.

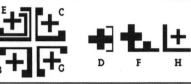

Solution
1: F, 2: A, 3: D,
4: B, 5: C, 6: E

Solution
1: E, 2: B, 3: A,
4: F, 5: C, 6: D

Solution
Pieces A and
D belong to
a different
interlacing.

PAGE 66

Solution
1: D, 2: C, 3: F,
4: B, 5: E, 6: A

Dice games

Solution

His first die shows a value of at least 3.

Explanation

The dice of the first player are worth either 1 and 2, 2 and 4, or 3 and 6.

Therefore a maximum total of 9. So in order to say this Paskal has already thrown at least a 3.

Solution

Laorans' adversary has thrown two ones and his first die is worth 5.

Explanation

Given Laorans' declaration, the possible results for the two players are:

2 for Paskal and 6 for Laorans,
or 3 for Paskal and 9 for Laorans,
or 4 for Paskal and 12 for Laorans.

Loarans' declaration means that, even if he throws a 1, he will triple Paskal's score. He thus has a 5 and Paskal a double 1.

Solution

Laorans means that if he throws a six, he will quadruple Paskal's score, because the value of his first die is equal to Paskal's score,

which thus must be 2.

Explanation

If we call the value of Laorans' first die T_1 and the value of the second die T_2, his total score $(T_1 + T_2)$ T and Paskal's score P, then:

$T_1 + 3T_1 = 4P$ thus $4T_1 = 4P$
$T_1 = P$

$T_1 + T_2 = T = 4P$ means that P is between 2 and 4.
The only possible solution is that Paskal has thrown two ones and that Laorans, after throwing a 2, throws a 6.
(P = 2, T_1 = 2 and T_2 = 6: only possible solution)

Solution

His die is worth 2.

Explanation

If P is the value of the die that Paskal doesn't throw again, and T the value of Laorans' two dice, then we have the following 2 equations:

$P + 4 = 2T$
$P + 1 = T$
by subtracting the second equation from the first:

$T = 3$

And thus $P + 4 = 6$ and $P + 1 = 3$ thus $P = 2$

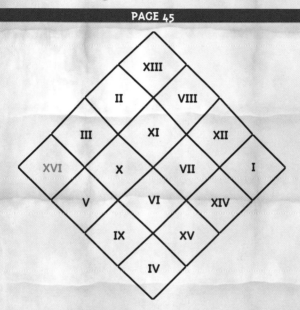

Solution

= XVI

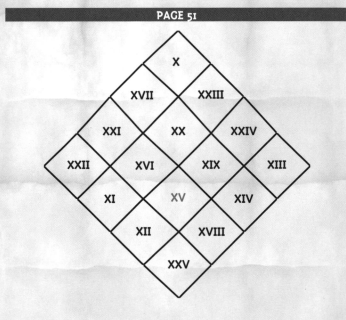

Solution
 = XV

Change

Solution

The total value of the coins in his purse is 6: the first coin is worth 2 and the second coin 4.

2 ( + ) = 12

 ×  ×  =  +

 +  = 6

 ×  ×  = 6, so  = 2 and  = 4

Solution

The total value of the coins in his purse is 10: the first coin is worth 2 and the second coin 8.

 −  = 6 so  = 6 +

 +  +  +  +  =  +  so 4  =

4  = 6 +  so 3  = 6

And therefore  = 2 and  = 8

Solution

The total value of the coins in Cathbad's purse is 3: the first coin is worth 2 and the second coin 1.

Pantheon

Collection

Collection of animals

Pair no 2

I	6	6		4
I				4
	8	8		3
		5	5	3
	7	7		

142

Collection of jewellery

Pair no 7

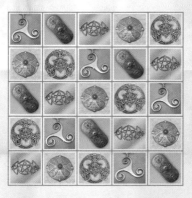

I	3	5	5	
I	3			2
8	8			2
		4	6	6
		4		

PAGE 80

Collection of heads

Pair no 1

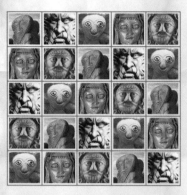

144

Collection of objects

Pair no 3

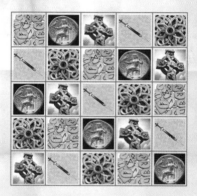

	8	8		4
6	6	7	7	4
	I			
	I	2		
5	5	2		

Collection of helmets

Pair no 6

	4		3	
	4		3	
	7	7	2	
5	5	I	2	
		I		

Celtic cross

Training

Solution

Alarig	21 years	Axe	20 hrs/week
Beltram	20 years	Sword	22 hrs/week
Gwennole	17 years	Lance	16 hrs/week
Malo	19 years	Club	24 hrs/week
Winog	18 years	Bow	18 hrs/week

Poems

Solution

Men	Women	Number of poems
Laig	Fiona	7
Malou	Eirlys	9
Quirec	Alastrine	5
Ruadhagan	Sezaic	4

Origins

PAGE 44

Solution:

Name	Place of residence	Type of house
Egarec	Scotland	Log cabin
Hingrad	Wales	Thatched cottage
Juvad	Brittany	Mud hut
Yaouen	Ireland	Stone house

Fairs

PAGE 60

Solution

Name	Site of the fair	Length of stay
Benedig	Lutetia	6 days
Kristell	Alesia	10 days
Rhiannon	Juliomagus	12 days
Ysolda	Burdigala	8 days

It all adds up

PAGE 4

Solution

Target 1 (18) + Target 3 (30) + target 4 (2)

Necklaces

Solution

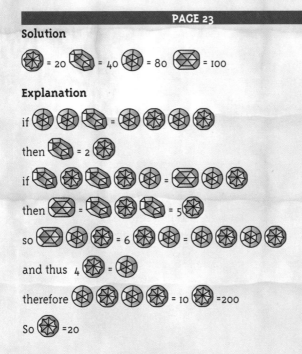

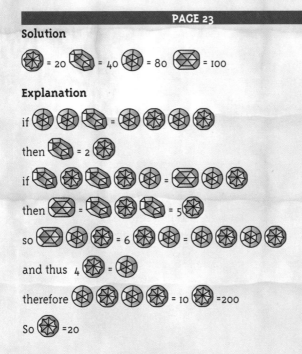 = 20 = 40 = 80 = 100

Explanation

if   =

then = 2

if   =

then =   = 5

so   = 6   =

and thus 4 =

therefore   = 10 = 200

So = 20

Magic square

Solution
N = I

■	III	II	IV	I
I	II	IV	■	III
IV	I	III	II	■
III	IV	■	I	II
II	■	I	III	IV

Celtic Enigmas

Only blue

1 dolerite and 59 rhyolites.

The Cromlech of Pou-Niairisson contains exactly 1 dolerite and 59 rhyolites, for the good reason that if there were 2 or more dolerites, the druid's second proposition would not be valid.

The influence of oral hygiene on cutting menhirs

No.

We know from (4) that druids who have bad breath don't wear a sagum. And these druids who wear no sagum, (1) tells us, don't drink fermented barley; but those who do drink fermented barley, according to (3), are the druids who have a moustache. And proposition (5) tells us that the moustachioed druids also have a beard, and (2) that the druids who cut menhirs are all bearded: consequently, a druid with bad breath doesn't cut menhirs.

You can't count on the wind

You have to take one of the vertical twigs in the first number and place it at the end of the formula to obtain:

XII–VIII = IIxII, or 12–8 = 2x2

The formula is now true mathematically, as 12–8 and 2x2 both equal 4.

Mouths to feed

That makes 4 sisters and 3 brothers.

The long march of Helix aspersa

Since the slug's speed is precisely 2 metres per hour, we know that one hour has passed. Consequently the snail, whose speed is 5 metres an hour, has covered 5 metres: no need to investigate further.

The four daughters of druid O'March

5 years old, 6 years old, 6 years old and 7 years old, respectively.

First let's calculate the number of candles to blow out today.
Let B be the number of candles, in other words the sum of the ages of the four sisters.
As the three other sisters are older than Amy, four years ago they were also born and everyone was at least four years old, thus there were 4×4=16 candles fewer.
We can thus say that:
B-16=B:3 (since there were then three times fewer candles than today)
3B=B+48
B=24

What were the ages of the four sisters four years ago?
The sum of the candles, and thus the ages, was three times less, or 24:3=8 (or 24-16=8).

The possibilities of making 8 from the addition of 4 numbers are:
5 1 1 1
4 2 1 1
3 3 1 1
3 2 2 1
2 2 2 2

But if Amy is referred to as the youngest, the she doesn't have a twin sister: in which case there remains just one possibility,

namely 1 year old, 2 years old, 2 years old and 3 years old.
Adding 4 years to work out the current ages, we indeed obtain
ages which add up to 24: 5 years old, 6 years old, 6 years old, and
7 years old.
What a memory that Amy has!

The forged sickle

We shall randomly assign a number from 1 to 9 to each sickle.

First weighing: the druid places sickles 1, 2, 3 on one side of the set
of scales and 4, 5, 6 on the other.
One of two things can happen: either a) the two trays will stay
level with each other, or else, b) one of the trays will be higher.

a) the trays stay level: this means that the faulty sickle is one of
the three others. All that then needs to be done is to weigh sickles
7 and 8: if one of the trays is higher, this will reveal the sickle
that the druid wanted to identify. If the trays stay level with each
other, the faulty sickle must be no 9.

b) one of the trays is higher: indicating that one of the three
sickles it contains is the faulty sickle. The second weighing
consists of following the same procedure with the sickles in that
tray as in the second stage of a).

The fibula calculation

Three fibulae cost 6 bronze coins, which means one fibula is worth 2 bronze coins.

If your first instinct was to subtract 100 from 112, thinking you would get the cost of three fibulae that way, you would have got 12, or 3 fibulae costing 4 coins each … and you would have been mistaken, because if the coat costs 100 coins more than the 3 fibulae, it would in that case cost 112 coins, and the full piece of clothing would come to 112 + 12 = 124 bronze coins.

The complete coat includes the three fibulae, so you need to divide the result of the subtraction (112-100) by 2.

Amicable divorce

Lips

The courage of Enora

69 days.

At the end of the 68th night, Enora will have covered a total of 68 league. At the end of the next day, the 5 more leagues she will have travelled will mean that she has covered the 72 leagues that separate the couple.
It will thus take 69 days and not one more for Enora to squeeze her

Efflam between her arms, with biceps out to here.

Show me the money

100 coins.

If 40 enamellers produce 400 coins in 4 days, 20 enamellers produce 200 coins in 4 days, so in 2 days, 20 enamellers will produce 100 coins.

The home of the true

One's word

The captain's age

The captain of the boat shuttle is 36 years old.

In effect, the druid sets up one relationship between the 60 years of age he is now with the age of the bargeman at a previous time, an age that is presented as 60 divided by 5, or 12 years old.

At the same time, the druid sets up another relationship, one of discrepancy or difference between, on the one hand, his age at a previous time (which we don't know) and his current age (x-60), and on the other hand the age of the bargeman at the same previous time and his current age (which we don't know) (12-y).

Whenever there's an age difference between two people, it always

157

stays the same, whatever length of time passes: we can thus assume that x-60 = 12-y.

But what we also know in this particular case is that these two unknown ages are the same, since the druid says: 'when I was the age you are now'. Therefore: x = y.

Which lets us reformulate the equation we have just put forward:
x-60 = 12-x
x+x = 60+12
2x = 72
x = 36

Family numbers

There are ten.
The father, the mother, the seven sisters and the brother.

Giant!

A pen and piece of paper will do the job for you just as well as the druid's piece of leather and whichever writing implement he uses to make a mark.

Place the point of your pen in the middle of the sheet of paper, and with your other hand fold over the section of paper on the left, so that the edge touches the point. Let's call the surface the point of the pen is on the 'good' side, and the surface next to it produced by the fold the 'bad' side (in fact, it's just the reverse).

Trace a circle on the 'good' side and, when your pen comes back to its starting point, without lifting the nib, move it to the 'bad' side and draw whatever kind of line you like until you reach the 'good' side of the sheet again, where you will draw a second circle, quite far away from the first.

When you have finished, unfold the paper: you have drawn the two menhirs, without ever lifting your pen, and the path or line that joined them has disappeared.

A gigantic achievement, is it not?

PAGE 26
Half true

This country counts using Roman numerals. Write IX to represent 9, divide it in half with a horizontal line, and the top half will read IV, which is to say: 4.

PAGE 30
No quarter

7 hrs 50 mins

In 15 hours, the teams can make 3 cages that each hold 8 Romans, 5 cages that each hold 4 Romans, and 6 cages that each hold 3 Romans, or 15 hours for (24+20+18) = 62 Romans, or 900 minutes for 62 Romans.

(900/62) x 31 = 450 minutes, or 7 hours and 50 minutes.

159

Chain reaction

It will take them 12 days.

The quickest method in effect is to saw open the 6 links of one of the chains and use them to join the 7 remaining chains together: so 6 days to open the chains, plus 6 days to weld them close.

Lawfully wedded

If the druid's wife is his widow, then the druid is dead: this is an obstacle that's hard to avoid taking into consideration.

Written by the wind

Two to three hours, the time to digest.

Cost of the menhir

They had a treasury of 125 staters.

Let x be the amount in the kitty prior to the menhir operation.
$$45 \text{ staters} = 1/5x + [1/5(x-1/5x)]$$
$$= 1/5x + 1/5x - 1/25x$$
$$= 2/5x - 1/25x$$
$$= 10/25x - 1/25x$$
45 staters = 9/25x
1125 staters = 9x

x = 1125:9 = 125

Bottoms up

There is the equivalent of barely five and a half goblets of mare's milk in the goatskin, the rest is water.

The first time she drank a goblet of the milk, there were eleven-twelfths of the litre and a half left in the goatskin. The second time, she leaves eleven-twelfths of the contents once again, but as a percentage of the mare's milk, it's eleven-twelfths of eleven-twelfths, which is to say eleven-twelfths squared.
The third time, there's eleven-twelfths cubed left … and the ninth and last time she takes a drink, eleven-twelfths to the power of 9.

Your abacus will tell you that 11 to the power of 9 = 238152716791 and that 12 to the power of 9 = 5211378155552. Dividing the first by the second, you get 0.45. 45% of 12 goblets comes to about 5 and a half goblets (5.4 goblets).

<hr>

PAGE 57

A lot from a little

A hole.

<hr>

PAGE 64

The inseparables

Two of the brothers leave on horseback while the third leaves on foot.
After an hour, the horse stops and sets down one of the riders. He is 2 leagues from their destination, and on foot he will arrive there in an hour.
Meanwhile, the second brother goes back to fetch the third brother, who has already covered almost 2 leagues. They leave again together and can even allow themselves a break to arrive at the same time as the first brother, who has travelled for two hours without stopping.

PAGE 65

Procession of bugs

'And yet ... they're going round in circles!' Gandalf might have said: because if they are telling the truth, it's because the bugs are not moving along the wand, towards the light or away from it, but around it.

PAGE 68

Myrdhin's precious stones

All Myrdhin can buy with his 130 staters is: one stone worth one stater, then two worth two staters, then five worth five staters, then ten worth ten staters: in other words, he will bring back one tourmaline, two topazes, five amethysts and ten diamonds.

PAGE 69

By Belenus!

Nowhere.
Survivors aren't dead, by definition, and, secondarily, by Belenus.

PAGE 72

To each their own

Sengann's wife is Ann.

Sláine's wife can be easily discovered through a process of deduction:

a) it isn't Raymonde,
b) it isn't Peggy, who is Genann's wife,
a) and c): it isn't Ann,
a) and d): it isn't Mauricette.
We can thus deduce that Sláine has married Maggy.

From this we know that Sengann's wife is neither Maggy, nor Peggy.

Moving now to Rudraige's wife, who is also neither Maggy, nor Peggy:
e) it isn't Ann,
a) and d): it isn't Raymonde.
As a result, Rudraige's wife is Mauricette.

Since Raymonde is neither the wife of Genann, nor Sláine, nor Rudraige, we need to ask which of the two others she has married:
a) and c): Raymonde isn't Sengann's wife, so she must be Gann's.

It is thus with his own wife, Ann, that Sengann romps.

PAGE 74

Rearing chickens

It will still take three weeks.
The hatching period doesn't depend on the number of chickens or cages.

PAGE 75

Topless priestess

Nothing.
The priestess is, quite simply, bald.
Topless then to the tips of her ears!

PAGE 76

Hot potato

A box — the coffin kind!

PAGE 79

Bog off!

49 days.
Since the surface area of each lily pad doubles every day, on the 49th day each of the lily pads has covered half the pond.

PAGE 81

Calcium for the agriculturist

Joseph MacBowen is a farmer, and he keeps goats.

PAGE 83

In moderation

Take the second full skull and pour its contents into the fifth skull, which is to say the first of the empty skulls, and return it to its place. Do the same thing with the fourth full skull, which you pour into the seventh skull in the row.
You will indeed obtain a perfect alternation of full skulls and

You will indeed obtain a perfect alternation of full skulls and empty skulls, without having touched more than two skulls. Cheers!

PAGE 84

The soft sound of the egg

Fanch knows that the hard-boiled egg no longer contains any liquid or semi-liquid matter that might oppose an inertial force. He will therefore spin the eggs with a nimble flick of the thumb and index finger: the one that spins quickest is the one he should take.

PAGE 85

The five Bituriges

The five Celts are sisters.

PAGE 86

Memory gap

1392
2 is the double of 1, 3 is a third of 9, and the sum of the four numbers is indeed 15, or the number of digits on two hands plus one foot.

PAGE 89

Shilly-shallying

Sitting at the table are a grandfather, father and son: according to their position in the family in relation to each other, this does

indeed make two fathers and two sons. There are thus three of them, plus the mistress of the house, sharing the pie, which makes four pieces. He has counted correctly.

PAGE 92

No hands, no abacus

You need to remove one of the vertical twigs in the first number and place it over the 'minus' sign to get:

I+IV=V

PAGE 93

Head and feet

MacBowen has 2 chickens and 7 pigs.

No doubt the druid isn't familiar with xs and ys, but would nevertheless be able to explain to you that it's a problem with two unknown quantities:
the number of laying hens (let's call them 'cluckcluck')
and the number of pigs (let's call them 'oink').

a) in the matter of heads, since each animal has only one, we know that:
cluckcluck + oink = 9

b) when it comes to the feet, since a chicken has 2 of them and a pig has 4, we know that:
2cluckcluck + 4oink = 32

c) let's reformulate a) as:
cluckcluck = 9 − oink

d) let's then reformulate b), and we can calculate:
2 (9 − oink) + 4oink = 32
18 − 2oink + 4oink = 32
2oink = 32 − 18 = 14
oink = 7

e) now that we've worked out the number of pigs, lets move on to the chickens by reformulating c):
cluckcluck = 9 − oink = 9 − 7
cluckcluck = 2

PAGE 96

Well spotted, blind fellow!

It's enough to see the crown with red berries on one of the heads to know that both of the others are wearing a crown without berries.

The blemmye correctly guesses that if his two companions of fortune, who can clearly see what's what despite their respective handicaps, haven't said anything, it's because neither the one nor the other can see anything but two crowns without any red berries, without for all that being able to guess what was on their own head.

On the other hand, their mutual silence allows the third party here, namely the blemmye, to work out by a cross-referencing process that he himself isn't wearing the red and green crown: le druid has taken the three crowns without berries out of his pouch.

The blemmye can thus give the correct response.

Utopia?

The blemmye's house is an igloo, quite circular and built from bricks of pure ice, located right on the North Pole.

Uchronia?

The dictionary

Breton removalists

The two pillars weigh 60 and 100 tonnes respectively, and the table stone weighs 140 tonnes.

If we call each of these pieces x, y and z, we can posit these three equations:

a) $x + y + z = 300$
b) $x = \frac{1}{4}(y + z)$
c) $z = x + y - 20$, thus $y = z - x + 20$

we can thus reformulate the first equation a) as:

$x + z - x + 20 + z = 300$
$2z = 280$
$z = 140$

this $x + y = 160$
which we can rephrase as follows, using b):
$\frac{1}{4}(y + z) + y = 160$
$y + z + 4y = 640$
$5y = 640 - z = 640 - 140 = 500$
$y = 100$
thus $x = 300 - (140 + 100) = 60$

The spendthrift druid

Before each purchase, the druid has a certain number x of stones, and after each purchase he has a number y of stones left. His expenditure corresponds to half of x, to which 5 stones must be added: $x/2 + 5$.

We can thus posit:
$x - (x/2 + 5) = y$
$x - x/2 - 5 = y$
$x/2 = y + 5$
$x = 2y + 10$

Let's consider his last purchase. He has nothing left over: the value of y is thus nothing, $y = 0$.
The formula $x = 2y + 10$ is thus equivalent to: $x = 10$.
The number of stones the druid had to buy the braces is thus 10 (which is expensive for a pair of braces, but remember these aren't your grandpa's Mickey Mouse braces but the Braces of William, so do you mind?).

* From this point, using the same principle, we can calculate the state of his purse when he bought the Cauldron of the Dagda, since y is then worth 10: x = 20 + 10, the druid had 30 stones (and he thus paid 20 stones for the cauldron)
* when he bought the Sword:
x = 60 + 10, he had 70 in his pocket
* when he bought the Spear:
x = 140 + 10, he had 150 left in his purse
* and when he bought the Stone of Fál:
x = 300 + 10.
The druid thus left with 310 precious stones.

PAGE 103
Stuff and nonsense

It will take them two hours.
In two hours, Konan will have made a third of the haggis, and Konogan two thirds.

PAGE 104
Dunces

That makes 11 bards without their lyres.

50 - 30 = 20 initiates who have a lyre, and these are all bards.
31 bards minus 20 = 11 bards without a lyre.

Daddy's girl

Pim is the favourite, with a fibula that cost her father 17 bronze coins.

The most expensive present is the one the druid gives Pim, since when its price is subtracted from the total, you get the smallest amount.

If the fibula given to Pim is x, y is the fibula given to Pam, z the fibula given to Poum and w the fibula given to Zézette:
if we add together $(x+y+z) + (x+y+w) + (x+z+w) + (y+z+w)$, we can see that we get each of the values times 3 $(3x+3y+3z+3w)$.
We can then add together the four totals $(38+37+28+27)$ and divide the total by three, and we know how much the druid spent in total: $132/3 = 44$ bronze coins.
All we then need to do is subtract the total of the other three fibula, 27 pieces, to work out the price of Pim's present: 17 pieces.

The hydra of Loch Breux

28 serpent heads

Whichever half of the serpent is cut (the top half, with the head, or the bottom half, whose head is already on the ground), we have to work out the problem starting from the end: before the third fight, there were three and a half serpents left on the monster's body, multiplied by 2, so 7 serpents.
Before the second fight, the monster had $(7+½) \times 2 = 15$ left.

And before the first fight, the monster was crowned with $(15+\frac{1}{2}) \times 2 = 31$ serpents.

From this total we need to substract the monster's remaining heads: $31 - 3 = 28$.

PAGE 109

Amuse-gueules

Dagon is Bajocasse (let's say he lives in the Bayeux area).

If the druid who has the fewest nuggets has x number of them, the others have, respectively, 2x, 4x, and 8x.

But if Gaston has 23 more than Fezig, Fezig has 23 less than Gaston: and in the sequence [x, 2x, 4x, 8x], Fezig can't occupy the last position, since Gaston has twice what he brought, but he can't be in the 4x position either, because 23 divided by 2 doesn't give a whole number …

Which reasoning also obviously applies to 2x.

Fezig's total number of nuggets is thus 23, and he is Lexovii.

Gaston has 46 and he's Veneti. Dagon has 92, he's Bajocasse. And the delegate of the Osismii, Edern, has brought 184.

PAGE 111

Double paradox

Transparency, or darkness

PAGE 112

Featherweight

The menhir weighed 350 tonnes.

Let x be the weight of the menhir. We can say that
$x = 4/7$ of $x + 150$ t
$x - 4/7$ of $x = 150$ t
$7x - 4x = 1050$ t
$x = 350$ t

Balls!

The Viducassi army is made up of 152 men.

The army (y) has shared 200 fireballs between them:
¼ of y takes 2 balls
¾ of y-5 takes 1 ball
5 warriors take 3 balls.

200 balls = (2balls x y/4) + (1ball x (3y/4-5)) + 3balls x 5
            = 2y/4 + 3y/4 - 5 + 15
$200 + 5 - 15 = 5y/4$
$5y = 190 \times 4 = 760$
$y = 152$

(Let's check: a quarter of 152 took 2 balls, or 38 x 2 = 76 balls, three quarters of 152 minus 5, or (114-5) took 1 = 109 balls
109 + 76 = 185
plus the 15 in total taken by 5 of the 152 warriors =200 balls)

PAGE 114

A bed of menhirs

Keep it simple: begin by drawing two parallel rows of three
menhirs, ABC and DEF, so that AB, BC, BE, DE and EF are
equidistant.
Between the two rows, place a 7th menhir half-way up: we've
gone from 2 to 5 rows.
Now place an 8th menhir in the centre of the square ABDE, and a
9th one in the centre of the other square: you will get 5 new rows.

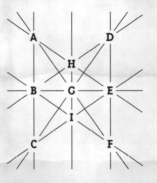

PAGE 115

Get your goat

The pens have to be built around each other: three pens, each
containing two goats, and the whole lot enclosed inside a larger
pen.

Slap happy

It's a team of 13 players.

If we take one of them at random, we can assume that he has slapped the palm of each member of the team, apart from himself, or T-1, T representing the team; the next one will have slapped the palm of all the rest, except for the one whose case we've just examined, because we're not little girls and we only slap once, plus himself, so T-2; and so on and so forth, until the last, who slaps the hand of just one other team member: $78 = (E-1) + (E-2) + \ldots + 1$ we then realise that to find the series to which we have to add 1, we just have to go in the other direction, adding until we reach 78:

$78 = [1+2+3+4+5+6+7+8+9+10+11+12]$

The answer is thus $12 + 1 = 13$ players:

$78 = (13-1) + (13-2) + \ldots + (13-12)$.

Fair share

Padraig should receive 6 pieces, and Quennegan 24.

3 litres in total have been drunk, or 1 litre per bard.
Padraig should be reimbursed for the 200 ml extra he contributed relative to the litre he drank, and Quennegan for the 800 ml extra. The relation between the respective reimbursement amounts being 1 to 4, the 30 bronze coins should be divided up along the same lines: 6 pieces for Padraig, and 24 for Quennegan.

The bard

He has 73 different songs in his repertoire.

Good accounts make good friends ...

20 kilograms

Explanation

If we call farmer 1, F1, farmer 2, F2 , farmer 3, F3 and P the total amount of produce:

$F_1 = 1/4\ P$
$F_2 = 5$
$F_3 = F_1 + F_2$
And
$P = F_1 + F_2 + F_3 = 1/4P + 5 + 1/4P + 5$ or $P = 1/2P + 10$

Therefore $1/2P = 10$ and they therefore have 20 kilograms to sell. The first contributes 5, the second 5 and the third 10.

Druids

None

Explanation

If we call peasant 1, P1; peasant 2, P2; peasant 3, P3; P the total amount of potion and X what remains after it is shared out:

$$P1 = 1/3P$$
$$P2 = 1/2P$$
$$P3 = 1/2P1$$

And

$$P = P1 + P2 + P3 + X = 1/3P + 1/2P + 1/2P1$$
$$\text{Therefore } X = P - 1/3P - 1/2P - 1/6P = P - (2/6+3/6+1/6) P = 0$$

Druid specialties

There were 120 druids.

The age of Glúingel

Eber Finn is 22, Eremon is 33, and Amergin, aka Glúingel, is 44.

Treasure

PAGE 24

🪙				I
I		I	🪙	
		2	🪙	3
🪙	I		🪙	3
I	I		2	🪙

PAGE 32

	2	🪙	
I	🪙	2	
3	3		I
🪙	🪙		🪙

PAGE 67

	🪙	2	🪙	I
🪙	2	3		
2			🪙	2
🪙			🪙	2
2	🪙	2	I	I

PAGE 73

I			2	
🪙	3	🪙	3	🪙
2	🪙	4	🪙	2
	🪙	3	🪙	
	🪙	3	🪙	

Published in 2010 by Murdoch Books Pty Limited

Murdoch Books Australia
Pier 8/9
23 Hickson Road
Millers Point NSW 2000
Phone: +61 (0) 2 8220 2000
Fax: +61 (0) 2 8220 2558
www.murdochbooks.com.au

Murdoch Books UK Limited
Erico House, 6th Floor
93—99 Upper Richmond Road
Putney, London SW15 2TG
Phone: +44 (0) 20 8785 5995
Fax: +44 (0) 20 8785 5985
www.murdochbooks.co.uk

Publisher: Kay Scarlett
Editor: Sophie Hamley
Designer: Camille Durand-Kriegel

National Library of Australia Cataloguing-in-Publication Data
Author: Ly Maguy, Masson Nicole, Caudal Yann Martin Pierre
Title: Enigmas Celtic / Maguy Ly ... [et al.]
ISBN: 978-1-74196-821-7 (hbk.)
 Series: Enigmas
Subjects: Puzzles--Celtic influences.
                  Amusements--Celtic influences.
                  Games--Celtic influences.
                  Psychological recreations--Celtic influences.
Other Authors/
Contributors: Ly, Maguy.
Dewey Number: 793.73

A catalogue record for this book is available from the British Library.

PRINTED IN CHINA.